Day Starters

Day Starters
Choose your thoughts, change your mind!

A collection of life changing affirmations, poetry, thoughts on creating, and philosophy of life and change.

David Sweet

Copyright ©2017 by David Sweet
All rights reserved. This publication contains the original work of the author, published here for the first time. All work is protected under the copyright and no part of this publication may be reproduced, stored in a retrieval system or transmitted in any way by any means, electronic, mechanical, photocopy, recording or otherwise, without prior consent of the author.

ISBN-13: 978-0-9983392-0-7

Published by
DAVID SWEET, INC
2005 70th Ave W
Tacoma, WA 98466-5540
Sweetcoaching@gmail.com
Sweetpoetry.com
(253) 565-7355

Printed in the United States of America

Book Design: Alice Briggs
Text Editing: Leslie J. Heineman
Cover: Robert Thompson

Acknowledgement

The author wishes to thank those close to him and the many others who offered honest insights in regard to this finished work.

Thank you all.

Dedication

Ode to Parkinson's

Gregory Wayne Sweet
November 9, 1966   August 22, 2015

He was a child of God, as are we all, and wore the badge with humility.

He gave his coat to a homeless man; he made and passed out sandwiches. Those in need were always welcome; he stood nonjudgmental and knew the power of forgiveness.

His spirit could fill a room, his voice an auditorium, and his laughter and wit any heart. He loved his family and his friends. He knew God, and he knew how it all worked.

Greg was gifted in many ways. He adapted, invented, and built; wrote, composed, and sang; and could see ahead to what the future required.

He had little or no fear and knew where he stood. He never had a broken bone or lasting injury from extreme sports or dirt bike racing.

He took lessons and learned to paint to gain advantage over the shaking. He studied and knew what was coming and what would be closing in on him. Yet he never lost an ounce of faith.

He left his heart for us. However, couldn't we all use a little help when the memories roll through and the wishing for one final glimpse, smile, kiss, or another chance to say and do more come over us?

Maybe what we didn't do or say is in the tears that hit the table, or somewhere behind the heart that strains from the hurt of loss and stretches to wish for just one more precious moment.

His last words on his way were, "Dad, I'm free."
Greg had "pinned it" one last time.

Reminder

Imagine you're on the trail—carefree and at one with nature—and with every step comes a growing sense of peace. The sun is bathing the forest, showering it with warmth as if to signal your arrival and to welcome your journey. The air is clear and clean, and your breath comes with ease as you start taking it all in. Chatty birds play hide and seek, staying just out of reach as they weave in and out through the towering old growth. The subtle, yet strong, hum of the forest and its busy creatures heightens the expectancy of an exciting day exploring. This is it—nature at her finest!

Then, from out of nowhere, it hits: A silent, overwhelming sense that you must stop. At that instant, deep inside you know that you're going no further. You're not moving, you're dead quiet, and your senses are racing.

What is it? What just dropped, and where? The sunlight still filters through the giants—that's not it. The birds have vanished, overriding any thought of coincidence. The answer has to be somewhere in the shadows—now seeming deeper, darker.

All that's living feels frozen, and what's left over, invisible and formidable, is leaning hard—very hard—on your soul. Your gut is telling you there's no choice but to back up, turn around so as not to disturb further, and leave. You take a deep breath, make yourself very small, and begin your exit.

How much presence does it take to sense, to quiet, and to listen?
How much trust does it take to know—beyond any shadow of a doubt?
How much courage does it take to alter a course, to turn back?

Bravo!

Table of Contents

Acknowledgement	*v*
Dedication	*vii*
Epigraph	*viii*
Table of Contents	*ix*
Foreword	*xi*
Preface	*xiii*
Introduction	*xv*
What's Here For You	1
Today	2
Affirmations and Assertions	4
Life Changers I	6
Life Changers II	10
Life Changers III	14
Life Changers IV	18
Bells	22
Black Ops	24
Centering	28
Claiming	32
Clarity	36
Communication	40
Edge of Courage	44
Hope	48
Knowing	50
Love Poem	54
Malpractice Explained	56
Miracles	58
Perspective	60
Pondering	62
Salute	64
Thoughts	66
What If . . .	70
You Can	72
About the Author	81

Foreword

When Food Network invited me to compete on season five of their popular show *Halloween Wars*, I knew I was in deep! Five teams of three contestants would each battle over five episodes for a grand prize of $50,000. (There was no prize for finishing second.) When my team met for the first time the night before the first episode, you could have literally sliced our combined anxiety with a chef's knife!

"Focus on your teammates . . . no one else exists," I explained. I asked my team simply to not look at any of the other competitors, and then asked them to do something special for me.

Just as they awoke, while still in bed, I urged each of them to list all the wonderful things in their life that made them feel grateful, and to thank the universe out loud. Then I directed them to visualize us winning, as if it had already happened. There could be no question of our team going to the finale, winning the grand prize, and celebrating all the dreams that the prize represented!

We actually surged to the finale and then won! Those steps we took to focus our energy and suggest the outcome to the universe I credit to David Sweet and the life strategies that he teaches.

As David says, focusing on success and telling the universe what you want leads all those distracting negative worries and anxieties to fade away. His techniques solve life's endless stream of problems and enhance the chances of getting the answers to our conflicts, problems, and challenges, and ultimately, the results we seek. After experiencing this in real time, I am a true believer!

Chef Robert Teddy
Executive Pastry Chef, Las Vegas NV

Preface

Consider: Panic attacks and paper bags
Valium and fuzzy-morning drugs
Agoraphobia and "don't go too far"
Sleep apnea and adrenalin rushes
PTSD . . .

Was it a heart attack? Luckily, David Sweet was only a few blocks from the hospital. The nurse came close, looked him square in the eye, and said, "Mr. Sweet, you should take a few days off."

"A fitting comment," David says now, "topping years of battling stuff rattling around inside. I'd had little success hiding 'it' and had found no real, lasting solutions, whether spiritual, professional, or medical-wise."

Soon thereafter, David began working with a Fortune 500 life coach practiced at "listening for guidance" (as David does). This listening greatly facilitates the coaching process. "During each of my coaching sessions," David says, "my needs were met even though they may not have been self-evident or spoken aloud. I trusted the process."

For David, it's been twenty-plus years of taking notes, rebooting, learning, practicing, rewiring, and rebooting again. David says, "You can learn to manage your thoughts, and you can have the skills to create your own experience."

These writings were created by David along the way. They contain insights on hope, courage, change, confidence, and truth. The affirmations, concepts, and thoughts put forth here will help you clear, center, prepare, and, regardless of the circumstances, to celebrate yourself—who you really are!

Introduction: Purpose and Goals of This Work

David Sweet believes that, no matter where you are in your personal or life circumstances, you can be better than you ever thought possible. Having the skill and courage to change, to manifest and discover more of who you are, and to exercise your inner power for a better life are within everyone's reach. As example:

Creating inside your being
vs.
"Making it happen"

The usual problem-solving methods include noticing, analyzing, concluding, acting on, and/or reacting to the situation. To make change through edict, or by whatever means necessary to achieve the "desired" goal, pressure the sale, or win at all costs, is often a recipe for the mediocre. Any coerced, forced, or one-sided solution ultimately stands a very good chance of failure. It will eventually unwind.

Imagine a surer, more powerful alternative of creating and goal achieving. By exercising and harnessing your innate power with feelings, affirmations, and visualization, you'll be able to achieve solid, permanent results. Whether business or personal, you'll facilitate and achieve the best solutions and outcomes for all concerned, including yourself. *Day Starters* will support you every day.

Day Starters

Carpe Diem!

What's Here for You?

Empowerment:
"to assist or enable someone to be stronger and more confident, especially in controlling their life."

Say good-bye to unwanted thoughts
Are you tired of feeling "stuck," faking it, or believing good happens only if you're "lucky"? Are you yearning to feel the excitement of new poise, confidence, and hope?

You can create for yourself; it's your life
Imagine positive events and a strong, inner peace as normal.
Feel yourself putting solid self-reliance and confidence to work.
Choosing your thoughts and creating your life is real power.

Day Starters . . . Personal empowerment
Dive in. You'll start to gain self-assurance right away.
You can go at your own pace anywhere—anytime.
Pick what calls out to you, and use what you choose!

Today

I remember who I am:
    My value is seen.
    Perfect timing is mine.
    I reflect before I speak;
    I speak the heart of it.
    Joy and enthusiasm are my hallmarks.
    My optimism and expectancy power change.
    Searching for truth erases mediocrity.
    Trust supports my vulnerability.
    Awakening rewards my perseverance.

I am reminded that:
    The only cost for thoughts are tolls paid
    on the way to truth and enlightenment;
    Anger pales beside love;
    Righteousness melts to freedom;
    Resentment stops at misunderstanding,
    proceeds to allowing, and ends with joy.

Today, I choose:
    Courage, hope, and confidence.
    Good health and mental resilience.
    Community and love.
    So be it!

Today

Streams of Consciousness
Random • Purposeful • Gut Feelings • Discoveries • Ahas • Celebrations!

Affirmations and Assertions

Affirmations and assertions are thoughts for inspiration that can be used to facilitate what you really want and how you choose to be. Part of the magic is your knowing what's right for you to use and when. The more you repeat an affirmation and imagine how the end results will feel and look, the more a positive change is supported.

Even if you don't know how it all works, start anyway. Fake it until you make it! You can say them to yourself or out loud, write them down, or treat them as prayers. However, you're free to choose. It's easy. Stay with it, and you'll soon notice your efforts paying off.

These affirmations and assertions are the result of David's own personal training, his one-on-one life coaching, and the custom workshops he creates for his clients. *Life Changers I* was written after a workshop with an investment/management team. Within three days of receipt, the team leader began reporting successes.

Streams of Consciousness

Random • Purposeful • Gut Feelings • Discoveries • Ahas • Celebrations!

Life Changers I

For One or For All

We're not available for scarcity thinking.
We're only available for abundance and well-being.
Nothing can stop us from reaching our highest potential.
Peace, joy, prosperity, and benevolence easily find us.

We're not available for malpractice from others or from ourselves.*
We're not available for thoughts no longer supporting us.
We're not available for thoughts no longer in our best interest.

Nothing can stop the right thing from happening.
Nothing can stop the right people from coming.
Those who come will be a blessing for us, and we a blessing for them.

No person or event can affect or diminish the essential me.
Tomorrow I'll awaken pain free, well rested, and alert with
clear thoughts.
I'll be able to see clearly and recognize the truth. I'll welcome
all change, blessings, and opportunities with gratitude
and thankfulness.

We stand clear and centered.
We call in all our sparkles, gather all our energy,
and take back and forgive ourselves for any mental malpractice we
may have directed at others or at ourselves.

* See *Malpractice Explained* page 56

Streams of Consciousness
Random • Purposeful • Gut Feelings • Discoveries • Ahas • Celebrations!

We're only available for good. Others may not do what we want
or believe as we do, however, no matter what, we'll be fine.
We stand ready in anticipation, expectancy, and allowing,
knowing in our hearts that all good will come.

We choose to be surrounded by empowering, positive, and nurturing
energy.
We honor ourselves with proper food and rest; and we celebrate our
new vitality.
We call in good health, positive support, community, fulfillment,
gratitude, and joy.
We welcome and accept what comes; we embrace it all, and we
give thanks.

So be it.
So be it.
So be it . . .

Streams of Consciousness
Random • Purposeful • Gut Feelings • Discoveries • Ahas • Celebrations!

Life Changers II

Empowering Language

Bringing multiple benefits to the user, the use of empowering language is a skill set of the successful Life Coaching system. How to start using it to your advantage follows.

Spoken words carry energy. The use of certain words disempower, signal confusion, and/or have an inner effect resulting in silent, negative energy coming from the speaker. Among the benefits of using empowering language are: manifesting and projecting positive energy and being recognized for the skillful use of more powerful word choices.

It takes willpower and commitment to notice and practice an empowering, articulate dialogue. As a reward for time invested in sharpening your language skills, you'll get to know more about yourself and notice a new confidence emerging. See page 12 for a sampling of words and expressions to avoid, and examples of positive, more empowering alternatives.

Streams of Consciousness
Random • Purposeful • Gut Feelings • Discoveries • Ahas • Celebrations!

Language Choices and Alternatives

Disempowering	Alternative/Own It!
Need	Choose, I choose
But	However
Why	What are your thoughts behind . . .
Want	I choose, I intend, I'm committed . . .
Can't	I don't choose to . . .
Just ("I'm just a . . .")	I'm a . . . (own it!)
Right ("Right?")	Leading the witness (good grief!)
Gotta ("I gotta go.")	I choose, I intend, I'm . . .
Should; shouldn't	I've decided, I've determined . . .
Have to	I've considered, and I choose . . .
I think/thought	I believe . . . (own it!)
Avoid "stupid," and "shut up"	How does name calling help?
But yeah . . .	Avoid slang; set yourself apart.
Are you a human "doing"?	Or, are you a human "being"?
Buy in (i.e., get them to "buy in")	Try sound, heartfelt logic . . .
You know . . .	Do they really know?
I'm not kidding.	Okay, so you're not kidding.

Hint for advantage: Upon noticing you've used a word or phrase you've chosen not to use, say, "I take that back" and then rephrase. It's clean, neat, and simple.

Streams of Consciousness
Random • Purposeful • Gut Feelings • Discoveries • Ahas • Celebrations!

Life Changers III

I'm a magnet for all that's good—I'm open and I allow.
Kindness and generosity easily find me.
I empower myself and others with positive thoughts.
If needed, I know others will come to my assistance.

Opportunities seek me out . . .
I stand in anticipation and expectation.
My talents are seen and appreciated,
And I'm generously compensated.

I honor and am true to myself.
My joy is mine, and no one can take it away.
I know gratitude is a practice, and I accept the challenge.
I stand in gratitude and thankfulness, and I see clearly.

I spread hope and joy as I go through life—the smallest word or action can uplift.
I stand in humbleness for all that I've been given and all the blessings and opportunities presented to me to serve others and the world in which we live.
I allow and forgive myself and others for any mistakes or missteps.
Whenever possible, I give more than bargained for.

I choose to grow inside and out with each passing day.
I observe, create, and listen with all my heart for the essence of it all.
I accept what is; however, I know I have the power to affect change.
I see what's real, adjust, and adapt with ease.

Streams of Consciousness
Random • Purposeful • Gut Feelings • Discoveries • Ahas • Celebrations!

Nothing can stop me from noticing my feelings and seeking the truth.
One of my strengths is noticing those thoughts that are no longer of use or benefit to me.
The ego knows only three dimensions, and I laugh in the face of any outdated thoughts.
I'm quick to tell such thoughts, "Go away, you have the wrong person," or "You're no longer wanted!" I celebrate my noticing.

Large or small—all my good efforts count and make a difference.
Imagining and then anchoring (i.e., owning) the feelings associated with realizing a particular goal allows me the advantage to achieve any goal faster.
I give myself love, appreciation, and great applause for my inner growth, clarity, and achievements.
I know who I am, and I claim it all!

So Be It.
So Be It.
So Be It . . .

Streams of Consciousness
Random • Purposeful • Gut Feelings • Discoveries • Ahas • Celebrations!

Life Changers IV

Nothing can keep me from the best outcome;
I'm always available for "possibility thinking."
I invest time in thoughts of potential,
and I delight in creating opportunity.

I'm a master at working inside myself.
What if everything I believe I know is false?
I release any attention on what I don't want,
and I hold my attention on what I choose.

"Good enough" is no longer acceptable; however,
for mistakes and missteps, I practice forgiveness.
I believe that "things must change for me to be okay" is false.
I know that power is not force or coercion over others
and that real power comes from awareness of thought.

Goodness finds me no matter what . . .
I know that I'm part of something bigger.
I do my part and believe that I'm never alone.
I'm not available for humiliation or coercion,
and I release any effect that past criticism
or shame may have had on me. (So be it!)

I release all thoughts that are limiting;
I'm not available for "victim stance."
I release all beliefs about having to always be right,
to control, to prevent, or that life is "risky."
To create, I allow, anticipate, and expect.

Streams of Consciousness
Random • Purposeful • Gut Feelings • Discoveries • Ahas • Celebrations!

Nothing can stop me from loving myself.
I'm truthful and generous with myself,
and I know that withholding my deep love costs me.
When extended to others, my love is felt by all . . .

Nothing can stop me from noticing;
I stand open, and listen with my heart.
I start where another's life is . . .
With gratitude and thanks, I celebrate them
and speak to who they are in that moment.

Streams of Consciousness

Random • Purposeful • Gut Feelings • Discoveries • Ahas • Celebrations!

Bells

Came the Dragon
Then came the Wind
The Universe grew silent
As particles dispersed
From the Dust
From the Mist
Past Time
Echoes came
And settled in
Loud at first
Trailing to soft . . .
As the bird
Lands in hand
Love mistakes not
And does not leave
Rejoice that you see
That which is yours
And
You
Deserve
It
All

Streams of Consciousness
Random • Purposeful • Gut Feelings • Discoveries • Ahas • Celebrations!

Black Ops

Whitewash
Deny
Spin
Blame
Rename
Resell
Repeal
Discredit
Distort
Ignore the facts
Drum it up
Pun it
"Buy in"
"Out it"
Soft-soap
Stain
Go around
Retread
Reconfigure
Circumvent
Trivialize
Discredit
Demean
Conceal
Of no consequence
Not significant
Make it disappear
With extreme prejudice
An accident
A leap of faith

Streams of Consciousness
Random • Purposeful • Gut Feelings • Discoveries • Ahas • Celebrations!

Years of experience
Dial it up
Turn your head
Drown it out
Shellac it
Erase it
Didn't happen
Not a trace
Who do you believe?
You have our assurance
You have our full cooperation
Believe us when we say
Our word is our bond
We throw meat to the lion
We mirror egos
We buy beliefs
We alter perceptions
We change minds
Next question please
How dare you ask

Streams of Consciousness
Random • Purposeful • Gut Feelings • Discoveries • Ahas • Celebrations!

Centering

Clearing

    Bidding farewell to any
    Lingering Chains of Doubt,
    Baggage of Fear or Resentment,
    I claim Freedom.

    Fretting and Regretting,
    Shame and Blame
    Have no place in my life;
    I gather and lock them away.

    Under the weight of my Resolve
    Judgment and Criticism collapse.
    I will not be denied Fairness,
    Clarity of Thought and Decisiveness.

I stand in

    Love, Joy, Gratitude,
    Good Health, Freedom,
    Fulfillment, Community,
    Embracing Change, and Discovery.

Summoning my Visions and Values

    Confidence echoing Skill and Tenacity;
    Persistence sparring with Adversity;
    Honesty and Truth crowding Deceit;
    Heartfelt Words and Courtesies multiplying;
    Permissions accepted and thanked;
    Listening and Intuitions ringing through.

Streams of Consciousness
Random • Purposeful • Gut Feelings • Discoveries • Ahas • Celebrations!

Feeling complete

    My Courage the Connection.
    My Values the Bond.
    My Service the power of suns—
    The strengths of each multiplied.

    I am open.
    I am ready.
    I welcome it.
    I claim it all!

Streams of Consciousness
Random • Purposeful • Gut Feelings • Discoveries • Ahas • Celebrations!

Claiming

Nothing left to grab onto?
Where could hope be hiding?
Is it behind the blackness?
Is it lost in the hollowness?

Can you assume it's available?
Can you expect and anticipate it?
What will finding it look like?
How will having hope feel?

Imagine the darkness lifting:
Visibility piercing a dense fog,
A hard winter bowing to spring,
A new dawn spreading warmth.

What of the smells:
Can you remember the scent of love?
Fragrances linger . . .
These past feelings of joy are yours.

Feel yourself breaking through,
Recounting, and reliving inside.
Pull the laughter, the glances,
And cherished moments back.

Streams of Consciousness
Random • Purposeful • Gut Feelings • Discoveries • Ahas • Celebrations!

No matter how trivial or fleeting,
All your past blessings;
The remembering, the calling back,
And all the joy are yours—a part of you.

Pull it all back, watch it come, and feel it!
Celebrate yourself and anchor* it all.
It's your tapestry, your cloth, your robe,
Your magic carpet of hope and joy.

It's available to energize;
To experience any time . . .
And it's all yours.

*(i.e., own)

Streams of Consciousness
Random • Purposeful • Gut Feelings • Discoveries • Ahas • Celebrations!

Clarity

Darkness
    If your light side isn't present
    Or feels beyond reach,
    Allow yourself the darkness.
    However, you have the power to notice
    And to hold this condition as temporary,
    Knowing deep down that it will pass.

Courage
    Inside, you are all-powerful.
    Take notice of anyone speaking to
    Or treating you in the negative.
    No matter how hard they try,
    Stand unavailable for any abuse.
    Your power is to mentally assert
    And vow that none of it will stick;
    In no way can it cling to your clarity.
    Watch it flow past like black water.
    Imagine it evaporating with each try,
    Down to the last drop, then gone.

Hope
    Imagine rays of hope shadowing darkness
    And waiting for you to call them forth.
    Hope will surround, comfort, and encourage;
    Nourishing your soul with expectancy.
    Hope brings truth, energy, and blessings
    To support and show who you really are.
    To believe is your power.

Streams of Consciousness
Random • Purposeful • Gut Feelings • Discoveries • Ahas • Celebrations!

Expectancy

> Where do hope, courage, and clarity originate?
> Are they like seeds, waiting and able to grow
> And manifest when needed and called upon,
> Or, are they always present and ready?
> What part does optimism play in being able
> To call forth these and other blessings?
> What part does expectancy play?

Celebration

> Your resolve and creativity don't go unnoticed;
> Congratulations echo through space and time.
> Applause and appreciation surround and embrace,
> Including a "thank you" from within . . . well done!

Streams of Consciousness
Random • Purposeful • Gut Feelings • Discoveries • Ahas • Celebrations!

Communication

Today I accept my responsibilities and the challenges before me.

To prepare, I honor myself;
Standing in who I am, centered and
Calling in silent moments, finding and
Confronting any worries, fears or doubts;
One by one I take these aside, lock them up and
Send them far away.

I assert: "I am not available
For fear or hostility,
Malpractice or coercion,
Deception or deceit."

I seek truth and clarity;
Listening to and acting on
My instincts and intuition.

I choose awakening;
Love, joy, gratitude,
Good health and freedom.

All those with whom
I come in contact
Will feel my energy.

Streams of Consciousness
Random • Purposeful • Gut Feelings • Discoveries • Ahas • Celebrations!

I stand before them,
Available and open,
Calling forth their goodness.
I give thought before I speak.
I speak the heart of it.

I speak to them—
To who they really are.

I welcome it all;
Trusting,
Allowing,
Accepting . . .

Nothing can stop me.

So be it!

Streams of Consciousness
Random • Purposeful • Gut Feelings • Discoveries • Ahas • Celebrations!

Edge of Courage

The edge of your courage is defined by you.
No one knows better who you believe you are at this time.

Choosing to grow; to have more of a sense
of who you really are, to be enlightened,
and wanting answers to questions deep inside . . .
That is the edge of courage.

To make the decision to call forth
change in your life, your thoughts,
and your consciousness . . .
That is the edge of courage.

To be willing to disregard old thoughts, habits,
and beliefs that no longer serve you . . .
That is the edge of courage.

Finding yourself in conflict with the old holding onto you;
tired thoughts and beliefs pulling at you
from places you never again want your mind to go,
and not giving up—continuing to stand firm
and wanting to know . . .
That is the edge of courage.

Streams of Consciousness
Random • Purposeful • Gut Feelings • Discoveries • Ahas • Celebrations!

When change has yet to come
and you're feeling all alone inside
and wondering what caused you
to start this quest for yourself,
and you don't let go, and won't back up;
clinging to the hope that you can . . .
That is the edge of courage.

When you're alone with your mind
feeling old thoughts, directions,
and inspirations crashing in,
dismantling, and mixing with the pain
of not knowing your future . . .
That is the edge of courage.

Streams of Consciousness
Random • Purposeful • Gut Feelings • Discoveries • Ahas • Celebrations!

Hope

**Holding
Optimistic
Positive
Expectations**

I claim that part of me that is hope.
Nothing can stop me from claiming my hope;
Nothing can keep me from it.

Passing through time, hope never leaves
And does not move when being sought out.
More powerful than any given moment;
It's always there—waiting.

Embracing it again,
I allow it to expand.
Feeling its power,
I remember it well.

I stand renewed,
Optimistic,
And expectant.
So be it!

Streams of Consciousness
Random • Purposeful • Gut Feelings • Discoveries • Ahas • Celebrations!

Knowing

The allure of darkness was enticing,
embracing, and tightening its hold.
Clinging to the edge of my heart,
I found myself gasping for air,
losing my grip, and becoming
more and more convinced
to let go and sink into it.

A hand reached out to me:
"You have many moments left.
Your soul will not give up on you.
No matter what the circumstances,
a part of your learning is to never let go.
You'll discover you can't, it's not you.

You can slip to the edge of darkness
and believe you're losing to the despair.
However, no matter what and at any time,
you have the power to call in the light—
to stare darkness in the eye.

Picture releasing those suffocating false beliefs
and deceptions now seducing you to join.
Your toll to pay is to not give up or give in—
rather to reclaim and rediscover who you are.
Can you recall the past goodness in yourself?

Streams of Consciousness
Random • Purposeful • Gut Feelings • Discoveries • Ahas • Celebrations!

Nothing can stop you from knowing who you are.
No person, no event, no place in time, no past enemy—
real or imagined—can affect or diminish the real you.
No matter how deep the chasm, how heavy the burden,
or how vivid the recollection—you will prevail.

You can banish any negative thoughts
no longer supporting you or in your best interest.
Notice them; assert that you're not available and
command them to go away, to disappear,
to sink out of sight, to drown in their blackness.
Imagine their void sucking them away.

Negative thoughts are not of you—
claim your power over them.
From the instant you notice them,
the advantage is forever yours.
They'll no longer control you.

Can you remember your joy, your laughter,
and those moments—large or small—
that are close and dear to your heart?
There's no cost, these moments are yours.
One by one, welcome their feelings back,
thank each for supporting you,
and celebrate yourself—all of you!"

Streams of Consciousness
Random • Purposeful • Gut Feelings • Discoveries • Ahas • Celebrations!

Love Poem

Dark clouds surrounded
Beckoning me in.

A ray of sunlight appeared
Followed by others;

Asking me to dance,
Bathing me in love.

I heard a soft voice;
Encouraging, understanding.

The clouds roll away
With the softness of your touch.

Dawn glows brighter
Knowing you are here.

Moonlight bathes the shadows;
Showing the truth of you.

I see you and
My heart knows . . .

I love you so.

Love Poem

Streams of Consciousness
Random • Purposeful • Gut Feelings • Discoveries • Ahas • Celebrations!

Malpractice Explained

Malpractice used in this context is negative energy originating from thoughts of malice or ill will. It can be negative thoughts coming from within as self-talk, or it can originate from others who are conjuring up bad thoughts toward you. Either way, it's negativity aimed at the positive side of your mental well-being.

The remedy is to send as much positive energy and as many good thoughts to others and to yourself as often as you can. Choose to mentally affirm and assert that you're not available for malpractice from others or from yourself. (Hint: Use this as an assertion each day, or if something's feeling wrong or heavy, you may be getting incoming malpractice from somewhere or inadvertently from yourself. Regardless, what's it worth to stay as clear as you can?)

Use the following assertion to clean up and clear away any mental malpractice you may have inadvertently sent out: "I take back any malpractice to myself or others, and I release any effect it may have had on me."

Streams of Consciousness
Random • Purposeful • Gut Feelings • Discoveries • Ahas • Celebrations!

Miracles

Does hope shadow miracles,
i.e., if there is no hope, miracles don't exist?
Are "small" miracles equal to "big" ones?
Do miracles noticed mean there is hope?
What defines a miracle anyway?
Is it our noticing that makes miracles,
or our hope that first pulls the miracle out to be?

Streams of Consciousness
Random • Purposeful • Gut Feelings • Discoveries • Ahas • Celebrations!

Perspective

Being close to the edge of life is a place our minds can go anytime.

When you're there, take all the missteps, have tos, "missed" goals, doubts, and can'ts, and mentally toss them to the surf's foaming edge.

Imagine the rest of your life as riding the waves, getting up and going again—a celebration!

It's having the courage to move forward not knowing when or how each wave will break. Regardless, you face the unknown . . .

Streams of Consciousness
Random • Purposeful • Gut Feelings • Discoveries • Ahas • Celebrations!

Pondering

Believing in miracles large and small . . .

Can you pause to look around and feel beyond yourself to your surroundings, to the land, to the entire earth?

Can you hold yourself as part of it, knowing there is a rhythm, a timing, and a purpose for it all?

Can you picture being everywhere; a part of it all and, at the same time, standing as one?

Can you imagine having the modesty to speak softly or the audacity and power to shout and be heard, not only by the earth but through all space and time?

Can you hold as a miracle the smallest raindrop, the babbling of the brook, the power and clarity of the sea, or the scent of rain?

What power trusts the old growths, rages with the tides, or silently announces spring with the first bud?

Can you stand quietly, go deep inside, and hold yourself as a miracle regardless of your circumstances?

Then you know peace and love; you know yourself.

Streams of Consciousness
Random • Purposeful • Gut Feelings • Discoveries • Ahas • Celebrations!

Salute

Today, dark clouds will dissipate for me.
Humbleness shall have no attachments.
My thoughts will center.
I'll be aware of all my good.
Standing free of ego and its
Distortions of thought,
I'll see the truth of all matters.
I'll be at one with the universe;
Open to reality in its entirety,
Judgment free,
Absolutely still,
And at peace.
Rejoicing and thankful
For all that I am
And all I've been given,
My heart will be full.

Streams of Consciousness
Random • Purposeful • Gut Feelings • Discoveries • Ahas • Celebrations!

Thoughts

Regarding lives, lies,
And choosing masters:

When you coerce,
Drowning begins.

When you hug,
You breathe again.

When you cheat or lie,
A new master arrives.

When you laugh,
Chains are broken.

When you judge,
You stumble and fall.

When you hold hands,
You skip into joy.

When you deceive,
Your path is erased.

When you love,
You're weightless.

Streams of Consciousness
Random • Purposeful • Gut Feelings • Discoveries • Ahas • Celebrations!

When you control,
You're compressed.

Allowing and accepting
Rewards with right timing.

Choosing vulnerability
Gifts you freedom.

Choosing to give credit
Recalls your grace.

Choosing to stand in truth,
Awakens future and past.

Can you remember:
Where you came from?
How you felt before?
How big you really are?

Streams of Consciousness
Random • Purposeful • Gut Feelings • Discoveries • Ahas • Celebrations!

What If . . .

The more you honor others,
The more you suspend judgment.

The more you use empowering language,
The more you'll learn to feel.

The more you work within yourself,
The more you'll quiet inside.

The more you practice listening—
The more confidence you'll have,
The more courage you'll have,
And the more you'll know yourself.

What If . . .

Streams of Consciousness
Random • Purposeful • Gut Feelings • Discoveries • Ahas • Celebrations!

You Can

You're standing in the rain,
However, don't feel clean.

Without the wind,
You must lean.

The blazing, taunting sun
Can't erase a frozen chill.

Darkness is falling:
Now you must squint.

The sun further threatens:
A black and white world.

The full moon struggles
Across empty tides.

Sound evaporates:
Remaining vibrations
Are a strain to feel.

The seas are on strike:
All energy is by land—
Great earthquakes.

Streams of Consciousness
Random • Purposeful • Gut Feelings • Discoveries • Ahas • Celebrations!

Volcanoes sucking air:
The earth must breathe.
Don't get too close.

Genocide landfills
Are at last dug up:
Tidiness ends here.

The world's hungry
Continue to affect all.
The earth wonders.

Fortunes are granted
To fill hollow insides.
Old echoes still hurt.

Birds begin their chorus,
Welcoming transformation:
New insights celebrated.

Walk as a guest:
You're not alone,
Not even in the closet.

Take a look around,
A good long look . . .
Can you go inside?

Streams of Consciousness
Random • Purposeful • Gut Feelings • Discoveries • Ahas • Celebrations!

Who are you really?
How capable are you?
Can you dig past the clutter?

You are in there,
With many great truths.
Can you search deeper?

Don't ever give up.
Hope is with you;
Sometimes it hides.

You have the power:
It's waiting for you,
Inside, past the dark.

Pull the curtain back,
Kick down the door,
Determine to find it.

In your darkest hour,
Can you light a candle,
And watch the flame?

However small, it exists.
However fleeting, it was.
Will the flame light again?

Streams of Consciousness
Random • Purposeful • Gut Feelings • Discoveries • Ahas • Celebrations!

For stepped-on souls
Burdened by untruths,
Old hurts burn at the base.

The middle is robust:
Spreading joy, laughter,
And thanks for being.

The top flicker breathes:
Growing in the moment,
Dancing with the future.

Can you hug yourself?
You are part of it all,
And can light it anytime.

You are powerful.
That is who you are,
And, you can!

Streams of Consciousness
Random • Purposeful • Gut Feelings • Discoveries • Ahas • Celebrations!